50 Coconut Recipes for Home

By: Kelly Johnson

Table of Contents

- Coconut Curry Chicken
- Coconut Shrimp
- Coconut Rice
- Coconut Macaroons
- Coconut Cream Pie
- Coconut Milkshake
- Coconut Custard Tart
- Coconut Flour Pancakes
- Coconut Chicken Soup
- Coconut Prawns
- Coconut Tapioca Pudding
- Coconut Crusted Fish
- Coconut Ice Cream
- Coconut Lime Chicken
- Coconut Rum Cake
- Coconut Granola Bars
- Coconut Banana Bread
- Coconut Cream Cake
- Coconut Chia Pudding
- Coconut Curry Vegetables
- Coconut Mango Smoothie
- Coconut Almond Energy Bites
- Coconut Caramel Flan
- Coconut Glazed Salmon
- Coconut Sweet Potato Casserole
- Coconut Cream Truffles
- Coconut Pesto Pasta
- Coconut Custard Pie
- Coconut Key Lime Bars
- Coconut Fried Rice
- Coconut Cilantro Lime Sauce
- Coconut Pineapple Upside-Down Cake
- Coconut Flour Brownies
- Coconut Curry Lentil Soup
- Coconut Cream Cheese Frosting

- Coconut Lime Shrimp Tacos
- Coconut Pumpkin Soup
- Coconut Lime Bars
- Coconut Crème Brûlée
- Coconut Sesame Chicken
- Coconut Tres Leches Cake
- Coconut Flour Waffles
- Coconut Ginger Carrot Soup
- Coconut Chocolate Chip Cookies
- Coconut Curry Tofu
- Coconut Lime Rice
- Coconut Cream Donuts
- Coconut Spinach Salad
- Coconut Chicken Satay
- Coconut Matcha Latte

Coconut Curry Chicken

Ingredients:

- 1 lb (450g) boneless, skinless chicken breasts, cut into bite-sized pieces
- 1 tablespoon coconut oil
- 1 onion, diced
- 3 cloves garlic, minced
- 1 tablespoon ginger, minced
- 1 red bell pepper, sliced
- 1 yellow bell pepper, sliced
- 1 can (13.5 oz / 400ml) coconut milk
- 2 tablespoons red curry paste
- 1 tablespoon soy sauce or tamari (for gluten-free option)
- 1 tablespoon fish sauce
- 1 tablespoon brown sugar or coconut sugar
- Juice of 1 lime
- Salt and pepper, to taste
- Fresh cilantro, chopped, for garnish
- Cooked rice or noodles, for serving

Instructions:

Heat coconut oil in a large skillet or pan over medium heat.
Add diced onion and cook until softened, about 3-4 minutes.
Add minced garlic and ginger, and cook for another 1-2 minutes until fragrant.
Push the onion mixture to one side of the pan and add chicken pieces. Season with salt and pepper. Cook until chicken is browned on all sides, about 5-6 minutes.
Add sliced bell peppers to the pan and cook for another 2-3 minutes until slightly softened.
In a bowl, whisk together coconut milk, red curry paste, soy sauce, fish sauce, brown sugar, and lime juice until well combined.
Pour the coconut milk mixture into the pan with chicken and vegetables. Stir to combine.
Bring the curry to a simmer, then reduce heat to low and let it cook for about 10-15 minutes, stirring occasionally, until the chicken is cooked through and the sauce has thickened slightly.
Taste and adjust seasoning if needed.

Serve hot over cooked rice or noodles. Garnish with fresh chopped cilantro. Enjoy your delicious coconut curry chicken!

This recipe serves about 4 people. Adjust the ingredients accordingly based on your serving size requirements.

Coconut Shrimp

Ingredients:

- 1 lb (450g) large shrimp, peeled and deveined
- 1 cup shredded coconut (sweetened or unsweetened)
- 1 cup panko breadcrumbs
- 2 eggs, beaten
- 1/2 cup all-purpose flour
- 1/2 teaspoon garlic powder
- 1/2 teaspoon paprika
- 1/2 teaspoon salt
- 1/4 teaspoon black pepper
- Vegetable oil, for frying
- Sweet chili sauce or mango salsa, for dipping (optional)

Instructions:

In a shallow dish, combine shredded coconut, panko breadcrumbs, garlic powder, paprika, salt, and black pepper. Mix well.
Place the flour in another shallow dish.
Working with one shrimp at a time, dredge each shrimp in the flour, shaking off any excess.
Dip the shrimp into the beaten eggs, allowing any excess to drip off.
Coat the shrimp in the coconut breadcrumb mixture, pressing gently to adhere.
Repeat with the remaining shrimp until all are coated.
Heat vegetable oil in a large skillet or frying pan over medium-high heat until it reaches 350°F (180°C).
Carefully add the coated shrimp to the hot oil in batches, making sure not to overcrowd the pan.
Fry the shrimp for 2-3 minutes on each side, or until golden brown and crispy.
Transfer to a paper towel-lined plate to drain excess oil.
Serve the coconut shrimp hot with sweet chili sauce or mango salsa for dipping, if desired.
Enjoy your crispy and flavorful coconut shrimp as an appetizer or main dish!

This recipe yields approximately 4 servings. Adjust the ingredients based on your serving size requirements.

Coconut Rice

Ingredients:

- 1 cup long-grain white rice
- 1 cup coconut milk
- 1 cup water
- 1 tablespoon coconut oil or unsalted butter
- 1/2 teaspoon salt
- 1/4 cup shredded coconut (optional, for added texture and flavor)
- Fresh cilantro, chopped, for garnish (optional)

Instructions:

Rinse the rice under cold water until the water runs clear. Drain well.
In a saucepan, combine the rinsed rice, coconut milk, water, coconut oil (or butter), and salt. Stir to combine.
Place the saucepan over medium-high heat and bring the mixture to a boil.
Once boiling, reduce the heat to low and cover the saucepan with a tight-fitting lid.
Simmer the rice for 15-20 minutes, or until all the liquid has been absorbed and the rice is tender.
Remove the saucepan from the heat and let it sit, covered, for an additional 5 minutes to steam.
Fluff the rice with a fork to separate the grains. If using shredded coconut, gently fold it into the cooked rice.
Transfer the coconut rice to a serving dish and garnish with chopped cilantro, if desired.
Serve hot as a delicious side dish to accompany your favorite main course.
Enjoy your fragrant and creamy coconut rice!

This recipe makes approximately 4 servings. Adjust the ingredients according to your desired serving size.

Coconut Macaroons

Ingredients:

- 3 cups sweetened shredded coconut
- 1/2 cup granulated sugar
- 2 large egg whites
- 1 teaspoon vanilla extract
- 1/4 teaspoon salt
- Optional: 4 ounces (about 2/3 cup) semi-sweet or dark chocolate chips, melted (for dipping)

Instructions:

Preheat your oven to 325°F (160°C). Line a baking sheet with parchment paper or silicone baking mat.
In a mixing bowl, combine the shredded coconut, granulated sugar, vanilla extract, and salt. Stir until well mixed.
In a separate clean bowl, beat the egg whites until they form stiff peaks.
Gently fold the beaten egg whites into the coconut mixture until fully combined.
Using a spoon or cookie scoop, scoop out portions of the coconut mixture and place them onto the prepared baking sheet, leaving some space between each mound.
Bake the coconut macaroons in the preheated oven for 20-25 minutes, or until the edges are golden brown and the tops are lightly toasted.
Remove the baking sheet from the oven and let the macaroons cool on the pan for a few minutes.
If desired, melt the chocolate chips in a microwave-safe bowl in 30-second intervals, stirring between each interval until smooth.
Dip the bottoms of the cooled macaroons into the melted chocolate, then place them back onto the parchment paper to allow the chocolate to set.
Once the chocolate has set, your coconut macaroons are ready to be enjoyed! Store any leftover macaroons in an airtight container at room temperature for up to one week.

This recipe makes approximately 20-24 coconut macaroons, depending on the size of your scoops. Adjust the ingredients accordingly for your desired yield. Enjoy these sweet and chewy treats!

Coconut Cream Pie

Ingredients for the Pie Crust:

- 1 1/4 cups all-purpose flour
- 1/2 teaspoon salt
- 1/2 cup (1 stick) unsalted butter, cold and cubed
- 3-4 tablespoons ice water

Ingredients for the Filling:

- 1 cup sweetened shredded coconut
- 2 cups whole milk
- 1 cup coconut milk
- 3/4 cup granulated sugar
- 1/4 cup cornstarch
- 4 large egg yolks
- 1 teaspoon vanilla extract
- 2 tablespoons unsalted butter
- Whipped cream, for topping
- Additional toasted coconut, for garnish (optional)

Instructions:

Preheat your oven to 375°F (190°C).
In a large mixing bowl, combine the all-purpose flour and salt. Add the cold cubed butter and use a pastry cutter or fork to cut the butter into the flour until the mixture resembles coarse crumbs.
Gradually add the ice water, 1 tablespoon at a time, mixing gently with a fork until the dough just comes together. Be careful not to overwork the dough.
Transfer the dough to a lightly floured surface and shape it into a disk. Wrap the dough in plastic wrap and refrigerate for at least 30 minutes.
Once chilled, roll out the dough on a floured surface into a circle large enough to fit into a 9-inch pie dish. Carefully transfer the dough to the pie dish, trimming any excess dough from the edges and crimping the edges as desired. Prick the bottom of the crust with a fork to prevent it from puffing up during baking.
Line the pie crust with parchment paper or aluminum foil and fill it with pie weights or dried beans. Bake the crust in the preheated oven for 15-20 minutes,

or until the edges are golden brown. Remove the pie weights and parchment paper, and bake for an additional 5-10 minutes, or until the bottom is golden brown. Remove from the oven and let cool completely.

While the pie crust is cooling, prepare the filling. In a medium saucepan, combine the sweetened shredded coconut, whole milk, and coconut milk. Heat the mixture over medium heat until it just begins to simmer. Remove from heat and set aside to cool slightly.

In a separate bowl, whisk together the granulated sugar, cornstarch, and egg yolks until smooth.

Gradually pour the warm coconut milk mixture into the egg yolk mixture, whisking constantly to prevent the eggs from scrambling. Return the mixture to the saucepan and cook over medium heat, stirring constantly, until thickened.

Remove the saucepan from heat and stir in the vanilla extract and unsalted butter until the butter is melted and fully incorporated.

Pour the filling into the cooled pie crust, smoothing the top with a spatula. Cover the pie with plastic wrap, ensuring that the plastic wrap touches the surface of the filling to prevent a skin from forming. Refrigerate the pie for at least 4 hours, or until chilled and set.

Once chilled, remove the plastic wrap from the pie and top with whipped cream. Garnish with additional toasted coconut, if desired.

Slice and serve the coconut cream pie chilled. Enjoy this creamy and delicious dessert!

Note: If desired, you can make a meringue topping instead of whipped cream. Simply beat 4 large egg whites with 1/4 cup granulated sugar until stiff peaks form, then spread the meringue over the chilled pie and bake in a preheated 350°F (175°C) oven for 10-15 minutes, or until the meringue is lightly golden brown. Let the pie cool completely before slicing and serving.

Coconut Milkshake

Ingredients:

- 1 cup coconut milk (canned or carton)
- 1 cup vanilla ice cream
- 1/2 cup shredded coconut (sweetened or unsweetened), plus extra for garnish
- 2 tablespoons sweetened condensed milk
- 1/2 teaspoon vanilla extract
- Whipped cream, for topping (optional)
- Maraschino cherry, for garnish (optional)

Instructions:

In a blender, combine the coconut milk, vanilla ice cream, shredded coconut, sweetened condensed milk, and vanilla extract.
Blend on high speed until smooth and creamy, about 1-2 minutes.
Taste the milkshake and adjust sweetness or thickness by adding more sweetened condensed milk or ice cream, if desired.
Once blended to your liking, pour the coconut milkshake into glasses.
If desired, top each milkshake with a dollop of whipped cream and a maraschino cherry.
Sprinkle additional shredded coconut on top for garnish.
Serve immediately with a straw or spoon.
Enjoy your refreshing and indulgent coconut milkshake!

Feel free to customize this recipe by adding a splash of coconut rum for an adult version or incorporating other flavors like chocolate syrup or banana for a twist.

Coconut Custard Tart

For the Crust:

Ingredients:

- 1 1/4 cups all-purpose flour
- 1/4 cup granulated sugar
- 1/2 cup unsalted butter, cold and cubed
- 1 large egg yolk
- 1-2 tablespoons cold water

Instructions:

In a food processor, pulse together the flour and sugar until combined.
Add the cold, cubed butter and pulse until the mixture resembles coarse crumbs.
Add the egg yolk and 1 tablespoon of cold water. Pulse until the dough starts to come together. If necessary, add more water, 1 teaspoon at a time, until the dough forms a ball.
Wrap the dough in plastic wrap and refrigerate for at least 30 minutes.
Preheat your oven to 375°F (190°C).
Roll out the chilled dough on a lightly floured surface to fit a 9-inch tart pan. Press the dough into the bottom and up the sides of the tart pan. Trim any excess dough.
Prick the bottom of the crust with a fork. Line the crust with parchment paper and fill it with pie weights or dried beans.
Bake the crust in the preheated oven for 15 minutes. Remove the parchment paper and weights, then return the crust to the oven and bake for an additional 5-7 minutes, or until lightly golden. Remove from the oven and let cool while you prepare the filling.

For the Coconut Custard Filling:

Ingredients:

- 1 cup coconut milk
- 1 cup whole milk
- 1/2 cup granulated sugar

- 1/4 cup cornstarch
- 3 large egg yolks
- 1 teaspoon vanilla extract
- 1/2 cup sweetened shredded coconut, plus extra for garnish

Instructions:

In a saucepan, combine the coconut milk, whole milk, and granulated sugar over medium heat. Stir until the sugar has dissolved and the mixture is just beginning to simmer.

In a separate bowl, whisk together the cornstarch and egg yolks until smooth. Slowly pour the hot milk mixture into the egg mixture, whisking constantly to temper the eggs.

Return the mixture to the saucepan and cook over medium heat, stirring constantly, until the custard thickens and coats the back of a spoon, about 5-7 minutes. Do not let it boil.

Remove the custard from the heat and stir in the vanilla extract and shredded coconut.

Pour the coconut custard filling into the pre-baked tart crust.

Smooth the top with a spatula and sprinkle additional shredded coconut on top for garnish.

Refrigerate the tart for at least 2 hours, or until set.

Serve chilled and enjoy your delicious coconut custard tart!

This recipe yields one 9-inch tart, serving approximately 8 slices. Adjust the ingredients accordingly if using a different-sized tart pan.

Coconut Flour Pancakes

Ingredients:

- 1/4 cup coconut flour
- 4 large eggs
- 1/4 cup coconut milk (or any milk of your choice)
- 1 tablespoon coconut oil, melted (plus extra for cooking)
- 1 tablespoon honey or maple syrup (optional, for sweetness)
- 1/2 teaspoon baking powder
- 1/4 teaspoon vanilla extract
- Pinch of salt

Instructions:

In a mixing bowl, whisk together the coconut flour, baking powder, and salt until well combined.
In a separate bowl, beat the eggs until smooth and slightly frothy.
Add the coconut milk, melted coconut oil, honey or maple syrup (if using), and vanilla extract to the beaten eggs. Mix well to combine.
Gradually add the wet ingredients to the dry ingredients, stirring until a smooth batter forms. If the batter is too thick, you can add a little more coconut milk to achieve the desired consistency.
Let the batter sit for a few minutes to allow the coconut flour to absorb the liquids and thicken slightly.
Heat a non-stick skillet or griddle over medium heat. Lightly grease the surface with coconut oil.
Once the pan is hot, pour about 1/4 cup of the pancake batter onto the skillet for each pancake. Use the back of a spoon to spread the batter into a circular shape.
Cook the pancakes for 2-3 minutes, or until bubbles start to form on the surface and the edges look set.
Carefully flip the pancakes with a spatula and cook for an additional 1-2 minutes on the other side, until golden brown and cooked through.
Repeat with the remaining batter, greasing the skillet as needed between batches.
Serve the coconut flour pancakes warm with your favorite toppings, such as fresh fruit, maple syrup, honey, yogurt, or nut butter.
Enjoy your fluffy and delicious coconut flour pancakes for a nutritious breakfast or brunch!

This recipe makes approximately 6-8 pancakes, depending on the size. Adjust the ingredients accordingly for more or fewer servings.

Coconut Chicken Soup

Ingredients:

- 1 tablespoon coconut oil
- 1 onion, diced
- 3 cloves garlic, minced
- 1 tablespoon ginger, grated
- 2 boneless, skinless chicken breasts, thinly sliced
- 4 cups chicken broth
- 1 can (13.5 oz / 400ml) coconut milk
- 2 tablespoons fish sauce
- 2 tablespoons soy sauce
- 1 tablespoon brown sugar or coconut sugar
- Juice of 1 lime
- 1 red bell pepper, thinly sliced
- 1 cup sliced mushrooms
- 1 cup baby spinach or bok choy leaves
- Salt and pepper, to taste
- Optional toppings: chopped cilantro, sliced green onions, red chili flakes, lime wedges

Instructions:

In a large pot or Dutch oven, heat the coconut oil over medium heat.
Add the diced onion, minced garlic, and grated ginger. Cook for 2-3 minutes, stirring occasionally, until fragrant and softened.
Add the sliced chicken breasts to the pot and cook for 4-5 minutes, or until lightly browned on the outside.
Pour in the chicken broth and coconut milk, stirring to combine.
Stir in the fish sauce, soy sauce, brown sugar, and lime juice. Taste and adjust the seasoning with salt and pepper, as needed.
Bring the soup to a simmer and let it cook for 10-15 minutes, allowing the flavors to meld together.
Add the sliced red bell pepper and mushrooms to the pot. Simmer for another 5-7 minutes, or until the vegetables are tender.
Just before serving, stir in the baby spinach or bok choy leaves, allowing them to wilt slightly in the hot soup.
Taste the soup and adjust the seasoning if necessary.

Ladle the coconut chicken soup into bowls and garnish with chopped cilantro, sliced green onions, and red chili flakes, if desired.
Serve hot with lime wedges on the side for squeezing.
Enjoy your comforting and flavorful coconut chicken soup!

This recipe serves about 4 people. Adjust the ingredients accordingly based on your serving size requirements.

Coconut Prawns

Ingredients:

- 1 lb (450g) large prawns, peeled and deveined
- 1 cup shredded coconut (sweetened or unsweetened)
- 1/2 cup all-purpose flour
- 2 large eggs, beaten
- 1/2 teaspoon garlic powder
- 1/2 teaspoon paprika
- 1/2 teaspoon salt
- 1/4 teaspoon black pepper
- Vegetable oil, for frying
- Sweet chili sauce or mango salsa, for dipping (optional)

Instructions:

In a shallow dish, combine the shredded coconut, all-purpose flour, garlic powder, paprika, salt, and black pepper. Mix well.
In a separate shallow dish, beat the eggs until smooth.
Dip each prawn into the beaten eggs, allowing any excess to drip off.
Coat the prawns in the coconut mixture, pressing gently to adhere. Repeat with the remaining prawns.
Heat vegetable oil in a large skillet or frying pan over medium-high heat until it reaches 350°F (180°C).
Carefully add the coated prawns to the hot oil in batches, making sure not to overcrowd the pan.
Fry the prawns for 2-3 minutes on each side, or until they are golden brown and crispy.
Use a slotted spoon to transfer the cooked prawns to a paper towel-lined plate to drain any excess oil.
Serve the coconut prawns hot with sweet chili sauce or mango salsa for dipping, if desired.
Enjoy your delicious and crispy coconut prawns as an appetizer or main dish!

This recipe yields approximately 4 servings. Adjust the ingredients based on your serving size requirements.

Coconut Tapioca Pudding

Ingredients:

- 1/2 cup small pearl tapioca
- 2 cups coconut milk
- 1/2 cup water
- 1/4 cup granulated sugar (adjust to taste)
- Pinch of salt
- 1 teaspoon vanilla extract
- Optional toppings: toasted coconut flakes, fresh fruit, mango puree, or whipped cream

Instructions:

Rinse the tapioca pearls under cold water and drain.
In a medium saucepan, combine the coconut milk, water, sugar, and salt. Stir until the sugar is dissolved.
Bring the mixture to a gentle boil over medium heat, stirring occasionally.
Once the mixture is boiling, add the tapioca pearls and reduce the heat to low.
Simmer the tapioca pudding uncovered, stirring frequently, for about 15-20 minutes or until the tapioca pearls are translucent and soft.
Remove the saucepan from the heat and stir in the vanilla extract.
Allow the pudding to cool slightly before serving, as it will continue to thicken as it cools.
Serve the coconut tapioca pudding warm or chilled, topped with toasted coconut flakes, fresh fruit, mango puree, or whipped cream, if desired.
Enjoy your creamy and delicious coconut tapioca pudding as a delightful dessert or snack!

This recipe makes approximately 4 servings. Adjust the ingredients accordingly based on your serving size requirements.

Coconut Crusted Fish

Ingredients:

- 4 fillets of white fish (such as tilapia, cod, or halibut)
- 1/2 cup shredded coconut (sweetened or unsweetened)
- 1/2 cup breadcrumbs (panko or regular)
- 1/4 cup all-purpose flour
- 2 eggs, beaten
- 1 teaspoon garlic powder
- 1 teaspoon paprika
- 1/2 teaspoon salt
- 1/4 teaspoon black pepper
- Vegetable oil, for frying
- Lemon wedges, for serving
- Tartar sauce or mango salsa, for dipping (optional)

Instructions:

Preheat your oven to 375°F (190°C). Line a baking sheet with parchment paper.
In three separate shallow dishes, prepare the breading stations: one with all-purpose flour, one with beaten eggs, and one with a mixture of shredded coconut, breadcrumbs, garlic powder, paprika, salt, and black pepper.
Pat the fish fillets dry with paper towels.
Dredge each fish fillet in the flour, shaking off any excess.
Dip the floured fish fillets into the beaten eggs, allowing any excess to drip off.
Coat the fish fillets evenly with the coconut breadcrumb mixture, pressing gently to adhere.
Heat vegetable oil in a large skillet over medium-high heat.
Once the oil is hot, add the coated fish fillets to the skillet, working in batches if necessary to avoid overcrowding.
Cook the fish fillets for 2-3 minutes on each side, or until golden brown and crispy.
Transfer the seared fish fillets to the prepared baking sheet.
Bake the coconut-crusted fish in the preheated oven for an additional 10-12 minutes, or until the fish is cooked through and flakes easily with a fork.
Remove the fish from the oven and let it cool slightly before serving.
Serve the coconut-crusted fish hot with lemon wedges on the side for squeezing.
Optionally, serve with tartar sauce or mango salsa for dipping.

Enjoy your crispy and flavorful coconut-crusted fish as a delicious main course!

This recipe serves approximately 4 people. Adjust the ingredients accordingly based on your serving size requirements.

Coconut Ice Cream

Ingredients:

- 2 cans (13.5 oz each) full-fat coconut milk
- 1/2 cup granulated sugar (adjust to taste)
- 1 teaspoon vanilla extract
- Pinch of salt
- Optional: 1/2 cup shredded coconut (sweetened or unsweetened)

Instructions:

Ensure the cans of coconut milk are well chilled in the refrigerator for at least 8 hours or overnight.
Place a large mixing bowl in the freezer for about 10-15 minutes to chill.
Open the chilled cans of coconut milk and scoop out the solid coconut cream that has risen to the top, leaving behind any liquid at the bottom. Transfer the coconut cream to the chilled mixing bowl.
Using a hand mixer or stand mixer, whip the coconut cream on high speed for 2-3 minutes until it becomes light and fluffy.
Gradually add the granulated sugar, vanilla extract, and pinch of salt to the whipped coconut cream. Continue whipping until the mixture is smooth and well combined.
If using shredded coconut, fold it into the whipped coconut mixture until evenly distributed.
Transfer the mixture to an ice cream maker and churn according to the manufacturer's instructions until it reaches a soft-serve consistency.
If you don't have an ice cream maker, you can pour the mixture into a shallow dish and place it in the freezer. Every 30 minutes, remove the dish from the freezer and stir vigorously with a fork to break up any ice crystals until the ice cream is firm but creamy.
Once the ice cream reaches the desired consistency, transfer it to an airtight container and freeze for an additional 2-3 hours to firm up.
Serve the coconut ice cream scoops in bowls or cones and enjoy its creamy and refreshing flavor!

You can garnish the coconut ice cream with additional shredded coconut, toasted coconut flakes, chocolate chips, or fresh fruit before serving, if desired. This recipe makes approximately 4-6 servings. Adjust the ingredients according to your desired batch size.

Coconut Lime Chicken

Ingredients:

- 4 boneless, skinless chicken breasts
- 1/4 cup coconut milk
- Zest and juice of 2 limes
- 2 tablespoons soy sauce or tamari (for gluten-free option)
- 2 tablespoons honey or maple syrup
- 2 cloves garlic, minced
- 1 teaspoon ground ginger
- 1/2 teaspoon chili flakes (optional)
- Salt and pepper, to taste
- Chopped fresh cilantro, for garnish
- Lime wedges, for serving

Instructions:

In a mixing bowl, combine the coconut milk, lime zest and juice, soy sauce or tamari, honey or maple syrup, minced garlic, ground ginger, chili flakes (if using), salt, and pepper. Mix well to combine.
Place the chicken breasts in a shallow dish or resealable plastic bag. Pour the marinade over the chicken, ensuring it is well coated. Cover the dish or seal the bag and refrigerate for at least 30 minutes, or up to 4 hours, to marinate.
Preheat your grill or grill pan over medium-high heat.
Remove the chicken breasts from the marinade, allowing any excess marinade to drip off.
Grill the chicken breasts for 6-8 minutes per side, or until they are cooked through and have grill marks, basting occasionally with the leftover marinade.
Once cooked, transfer the chicken breasts to a serving platter and let them rest for a few minutes.
Garnish the coconut lime chicken with chopped fresh cilantro and serve hot with lime wedges on the side for squeezing.
Enjoy your delicious and flavorful coconut lime chicken with your favorite side dishes or salads!

This recipe serves about 4 people. Adjust the ingredients accordingly based on your serving size requirements.

Coconut Rum Cake

Ingredients:

For the cake:

- 1 cup (2 sticks) unsalted butter, softened
- 1 1/2 cups granulated sugar
- 4 large eggs
- 2 cups all-purpose flour
- 1 teaspoon baking powder
- 1/2 teaspoon baking soda
- 1/4 teaspoon salt
- 1 cup unsweetened shredded coconut
- 1 cup coconut milk
- 1/4 cup dark rum
- 1 teaspoon vanilla extract

For the rum glaze:

- 1/4 cup (1/2 stick) unsalted butter
- 1/2 cup granulated sugar
- 1/4 cup water
- 1/4 cup dark rum

For garnish (optional):

- Additional shredded coconut, toasted

Instructions:

Preheat your oven to 350°F (175°C). Grease and flour a 10-inch bundt pan or tube pan.
In a large mixing bowl, cream together the softened butter and granulated sugar until light and fluffy.
Beat in the eggs, one at a time, until well incorporated.

In a separate bowl, sift together the all-purpose flour, baking powder, baking soda, and salt.

Gradually add the dry ingredients to the creamed mixture, alternating with the coconut milk and dark rum. Begin and end with the dry ingredients.

Stir in the shredded coconut and vanilla extract until evenly combined.

Pour the batter into the prepared bundt pan, smoothing the top with a spatula.

Bake in the preheated oven for 45-50 minutes, or until a toothpick inserted into the center of the cake comes out clean.

While the cake is baking, prepare the rum glaze. In a small saucepan, combine the butter, granulated sugar, and water. Cook over medium heat, stirring constantly, until the sugar is dissolved and the mixture comes to a simmer.

Remove the saucepan from the heat and stir in the dark rum. Set aside.

Once the cake is baked, remove it from the oven and let it cool in the pan for 10 minutes.

Carefully invert the cake onto a serving platter or wire rack. Pierce the top of the cake all over with a skewer or toothpick.

Slowly pour the rum glaze over the warm cake, allowing it to soak in.

Let the cake cool completely before serving.

If desired, garnish the coconut rum cake with additional toasted shredded coconut before serving.

Slice and enjoy this moist and flavorful coconut rum cake!

This recipe serves about 10-12 people. Adjust the ingredients accordingly based on your serving size requirements.

Coconut Granola Bars

Ingredients:

- 2 cups old-fashioned rolled oats
- 1 cup shredded coconut (sweetened or unsweetened)
- 1/2 cup chopped nuts (such as almonds, pecans, or cashews)
- 1/4 cup honey or maple syrup
- 1/4 cup coconut oil, melted
- 1/4 cup almond butter or peanut butter
- 1 teaspoon vanilla extract
- 1/4 teaspoon salt
- Optional add-ins: chocolate chips, dried fruit (such as raisins or cranberries), chia seeds, flaxseeds, or sesame seeds

Instructions:

Preheat your oven to 350°F (175°C). Line an 8x8-inch baking dish with parchment paper, leaving some overhang on the sides for easy removal.
In a large mixing bowl, combine the rolled oats, shredded coconut, and chopped nuts.
In a small saucepan, heat the honey or maple syrup, melted coconut oil, almond butter or peanut butter, vanilla extract, and salt over low heat. Stir until the mixture is well combined and smooth.
Pour the wet mixture over the dry ingredients in the mixing bowl. Stir until all the dry ingredients are evenly coated with the wet mixture. If using any optional add-ins, fold them into the mixture at this point.
Transfer the mixture to the prepared baking dish. Use a spatula or your hands to press the mixture firmly and evenly into the dish.
Bake in the preheated oven for 20-25 minutes, or until the edges are golden brown.
Remove the baking dish from the oven and let the granola bars cool completely in the dish.
Once cooled, lift the parchment paper to remove the granola slab from the dish. Place it on a cutting board and use a sharp knife to cut it into bars or squares of your desired size.
Store the coconut granola bars in an airtight container at room temperature for up to one week, or in the refrigerator for longer shelf life.

Enjoy your homemade coconut granola bars as a nutritious snack on the go or a quick breakfast option!

Feel free to customize these granola bars by swapping out ingredients or adding your favorite mix-ins to suit your taste preferences.

Coconut Banana Bread

Ingredients:

- 2 cups all-purpose flour
- 1 teaspoon baking powder
- 1/2 teaspoon baking soda
- 1/2 teaspoon salt
- 1/2 cup unsalted butter, softened
- 3/4 cup granulated sugar
- 2 large eggs
- 3 ripe bananas, mashed
- 1/4 cup coconut milk
- 1 teaspoon vanilla extract
- 1/2 cup shredded coconut (sweetened or unsweetened), plus extra for topping (optional)

Instructions:

Preheat your oven to 350°F (175°C). Grease and flour a 9x5-inch loaf pan.
In a medium bowl, sift together the all-purpose flour, baking powder, baking soda, and salt. Set aside.
In a large mixing bowl, cream together the softened butter and granulated sugar until light and fluffy.
Beat in the eggs, one at a time, until well incorporated.
Add the mashed bananas, coconut milk, and vanilla extract to the wet mixture. Mix until combined.
Gradually add the dry ingredients to the wet ingredients, stirring until just combined. Be careful not to overmix.
Gently fold in the shredded coconut until evenly distributed throughout the batter.
Pour the batter into the prepared loaf pan, spreading it out evenly with a spatula.
If desired, sprinkle additional shredded coconut on top of the batter for garnish.
Bake in the preheated oven for 55-65 minutes, or until a toothpick inserted into the center of the bread comes out clean.
If the top of the bread starts to brown too quickly, you can tent it loosely with aluminum foil halfway through baking.
Once baked, remove the banana bread from the oven and let it cool in the pan for 10 minutes.

Carefully transfer the bread to a wire rack to cool completely before slicing. Slice and serve your delicious coconut banana bread as a tasty snack or breakfast treat!

This recipe yields one loaf of banana bread, approximately 10 slices. Adjust the ingredients accordingly if you want to make multiple loaves or if you prefer a larger batch.

Coconut Cream Cake

Ingredients:

For the cake:

- 2 cups all-purpose flour
- 2 teaspoons baking powder
- 1/2 teaspoon baking soda
- 1/2 teaspoon salt
- 1/2 cup unsalted butter, softened
- 1 cup granulated sugar
- 2 large eggs
- 1 teaspoon vanilla extract
- 1 cup coconut milk
- 1/2 cup shredded coconut (sweetened or unsweetened)

For the coconut cream frosting:

- 2 cups heavy cream
- 1/2 cup powdered sugar
- 1 teaspoon vanilla extract
- 1/2 cup shredded coconut (sweetened or unsweetened), for garnish

Instructions:

Preheat your oven to 350°F (175°C). Grease and flour two 9-inch round cake pans.
In a medium bowl, sift together the all-purpose flour, baking powder, baking soda, and salt. Set aside.
In a large mixing bowl, cream together the softened butter and granulated sugar until light and fluffy.
Beat in the eggs, one at a time, until well incorporated. Stir in the vanilla extract.
Gradually add the dry ingredients to the wet ingredients, alternating with the coconut milk, beginning and ending with the dry ingredients. Mix until just combined.
Fold in the shredded coconut until evenly distributed throughout the batter.
Divide the batter evenly between the prepared cake pans and smooth the tops with a spatula.

Bake in the preheated oven for 25-30 minutes, or until a toothpick inserted into the center of the cakes comes out clean.

Remove the cakes from the oven and let them cool in the pans for 10 minutes. Then, transfer them to wire racks to cool completely.

While the cakes are cooling, prepare the coconut cream frosting. In a mixing bowl, beat the heavy cream, powdered sugar, and vanilla extract until stiff peaks form.

Once the cakes are completely cooled, place one cake layer on a serving plate. Spread a generous amount of coconut cream frosting over the top.

Place the second cake layer on top and frost the top and sides of the cake with the remaining coconut cream frosting.

Sprinkle shredded coconut over the top of the cake for garnish.

Chill the cake in the refrigerator for at least 1 hour before serving to allow the frosting to set.

Slice and serve your delicious coconut cream cake and enjoy!

This recipe yields one 9-inch layer cake, serving approximately 8-10 people. Adjust the ingredients accordingly if you need to make a larger cake or if you prefer cupcakes.

Coconut Chia Pudding

Ingredients:

- 1/4 cup chia seeds
- 1 cup coconut milk (canned or carton)
- 1 tablespoon honey or maple syrup (optional, for sweetness)
- 1/2 teaspoon vanilla extract
- Optional toppings: fresh fruit (such as berries, sliced bananas, or mango), shredded coconut, chopped nuts, granola, or a drizzle of honey

Instructions:

In a mixing bowl or jar, combine the chia seeds, coconut milk, honey or maple syrup (if using), and vanilla extract. Stir well to combine.
Cover the bowl or jar and refrigerate the mixture for at least 4 hours or overnight, allowing the chia seeds to absorb the liquid and thicken.
After the pudding has set, give it a good stir to redistribute the chia seeds evenly throughout the mixture.
If the pudding is too thick for your liking, you can add a little more coconut milk to reach your desired consistency.
Serve the coconut chia pudding in individual bowls or jars, topped with your favorite toppings such as fresh fruit, shredded coconut, chopped nuts, granola, or a drizzle of honey.
Enjoy your creamy and nutritious coconut chia pudding as a satisfying breakfast, snack, or dessert option!

This recipe makes approximately 2 servings. Adjust the ingredients accordingly for more servings or if you want to make a larger batch.

Coconut Curry Vegetables

Ingredients:

- 2 tablespoons coconut oil
- 1 onion, diced
- 3 cloves garlic, minced
- 1 tablespoon grated ginger
- 2 tablespoons red curry paste
- 1 can (13.5 oz) coconut milk
- 1 cup vegetable broth
- 1 tablespoon soy sauce or tamari
- 1 tablespoon brown sugar or coconut sugar
- 1 teaspoon curry powder
- 1/2 teaspoon turmeric powder
- 1/2 teaspoon cumin
- Salt and pepper to taste
- 3 cups mixed vegetables (such as bell peppers, carrots, broccoli, cauliflower, snow peas)
- Cooked rice or noodles for serving
- Fresh cilantro, chopped, for garnish (optional)
- Lime wedges for serving (optional)

Instructions:

Heat the coconut oil in a large skillet or wok over medium heat.
Add the diced onion to the skillet and sauté for 2-3 minutes until softened.
Stir in the minced garlic and grated ginger, and cook for another minute until fragrant.
Add the red curry paste to the skillet and cook for 1-2 minutes, stirring constantly to toast the spices.
Pour in the coconut milk and vegetable broth, stirring to combine.
Add the soy sauce, brown sugar, curry powder, turmeric, and cumin to the skillet.
Mix well until the sauce is smooth and combined.
Season with salt and pepper to taste.
Add the mixed vegetables to the skillet and stir to coat them in the curry sauce.
Bring the mixture to a simmer, then reduce the heat to medium-low and let it cook for 8-10 minutes, or until the vegetables are tender but still slightly crisp.

Taste the curry and adjust the seasoning if necessary.
Once the vegetables are cooked to your liking and the sauce has thickened slightly, remove the skillet from the heat.
Serve the coconut curry vegetables hot over cooked rice or noodles.
Garnish with fresh chopped cilantro and serve with lime wedges on the side for squeezing, if desired.
Enjoy your flavorful and aromatic coconut curry vegetables as a delicious and satisfying meal!

Feel free to customize this recipe by using your favorite vegetables or adding protein sources like tofu, chickpeas, or shrimp. Adjust the spice level according to your preference by adding more or less red curry paste.

Coconut Mango Smoothie

Ingredients:

- 1 ripe mango, peeled, pitted, and diced
- 1/2 cup coconut milk (canned or carton)
- 1/2 cup plain or vanilla yogurt
- 1/2 cup ice cubes
- 1 tablespoon honey or maple syrup (optional, adjust to taste)
- 1/4 teaspoon vanilla extract
- Optional toppings: shredded coconut, sliced mango, or mint leaves

Instructions:

Place the diced mango, coconut milk, yogurt, ice cubes, honey or maple syrup (if using), and vanilla extract in a blender.
Blend on high speed until smooth and creamy, scraping down the sides of the blender as needed.
Taste the smoothie and adjust sweetness or thickness by adding more honey, maple syrup, yogurt, or ice cubes as desired.
Once blended to your liking, pour the coconut mango smoothie into glasses.
If desired, garnish each smoothie with shredded coconut, sliced mango, or mint leaves for presentation.
Serve immediately with a straw or spoon.
Enjoy your refreshing and tropical coconut mango smoothie as a nutritious breakfast, snack, or dessert option!

Feel free to customize this recipe by adding other fruits like pineapple or banana for additional flavor. You can also incorporate protein powder, chia seeds, or spinach for added nutrients. Adjust the ingredients according to your taste preferences and dietary needs.

Coconut Almond Energy Bites

Ingredients:

- 1 cup rolled oats
- 1/2 cup almond butter
- 1/4 cup honey or maple syrup
- 1/4 cup shredded coconut (sweetened or unsweetened)
- 1/4 cup chopped almonds
- 1/4 cup mini chocolate chips (optional)
- 1 teaspoon vanilla extract
- Pinch of salt

Instructions:

In a large mixing bowl, combine the rolled oats, almond butter, honey or maple syrup, shredded coconut, chopped almonds, mini chocolate chips (if using), vanilla extract, and a pinch of salt.

Stir the mixture until well combined and the ingredients are evenly distributed.

If the mixture seems too dry, you can add a little more almond butter or honey to help bind everything together.

Once the mixture is well combined, cover the bowl and refrigerate it for 30 minutes to allow it to firm up slightly, which will make it easier to shape into balls.

After chilling, remove the bowl from the refrigerator. Take small portions of the mixture and roll them between your palms to form small energy bites or balls.

Place the formed energy bites on a baking sheet lined with parchment paper.

Once all the mixture has been rolled into balls, you can optionally roll them in additional shredded coconut for extra coating.

Transfer the energy bites back to the refrigerator and chill for another 30 minutes to set.

Once chilled, the coconut almond energy bites are ready to eat! Store any leftovers in an airtight container in the refrigerator for up to one week.

Enjoy these delicious and nutritious coconut almond energy bites as a quick and convenient snack for an energy boost throughout the day!

Feel free to customize this recipe by adding other mix-ins such as chia seeds, dried fruit, or protein powder. Adjust the sweetness by adding more or less honey or maple syrup according to your taste preferences.

Coconut Caramel Flan

Ingredients:

For the caramel:

- 1 cup granulated sugar
- 1/4 cup water

For the flan:

- 4 large eggs
- 1 can (14 oz) sweetened condensed milk
- 1 can (13.5 oz) coconut milk
- 1 teaspoon vanilla extract
- Pinch of salt
- Shredded coconut, toasted (optional, for garnish)

Instructions:

Preheat your oven to 350°F (175°C). Place a roasting pan filled with about 1 inch of hot water on the bottom rack of the oven. This will create a water bath for the flan.

Prepare the caramel: In a small saucepan, combine the granulated sugar and water. Heat over medium-high heat, stirring constantly, until the sugar dissolves. Once the sugar has dissolved, stop stirring and let the mixture cook undisturbed until it turns a deep amber color, about 8-10 minutes. Swirl the pan occasionally to ensure even caramelization.

Once the caramel reaches the desired color, immediately pour it into the bottom of a 9-inch round cake pan or flan mold, swirling to coat the bottom evenly. Be careful as the caramel will be very hot. Allow it to cool and harden while you prepare the flan mixture.

In a large mixing bowl, whisk together the eggs, sweetened condensed milk, coconut milk, vanilla extract, and a pinch of salt until well combined.

Pour the flan mixture over the cooled caramel in the cake pan.

Cover the cake pan tightly with aluminum foil to prevent water from seeping in during baking.

Place the covered cake pan in the preheated oven, directly over the water bath, and bake for 50-60 minutes, or until the flan is set around the edges but still slightly jiggly in the center.

Once the flan is done baking, remove it from the oven and carefully remove the aluminum foil.

Allow the flan to cool to room temperature, then refrigerate it for at least 4 hours or overnight to chill and set completely.

To serve, run a knife around the edges of the flan to loosen it from the pan. Place a serving plate over the top of the pan and quickly invert it to release the flan onto the plate.

If desired, garnish the coconut caramel flan with toasted shredded coconut before serving.

Slice and serve the flan cold, enjoying its creamy texture and caramelized coconut flavor!

This recipe yields approximately 8 servings. Adjust the ingredients accordingly if you need to make a larger or smaller batch.

Coconut Glazed Salmon

Ingredients:

For the coconut glaze:

- 1/4 cup coconut milk
- 2 tablespoons soy sauce or tamari
- 2 tablespoons honey or maple syrup
- 1 tablespoon lime juice
- 1 teaspoon grated ginger
- 1 clove garlic, minced
- 1/2 teaspoon chili flakes (optional, for heat)
- Salt and pepper to taste

For the salmon:

- 4 salmon fillets, skin-on or skinless
- Salt and pepper to taste
- 2 tablespoons coconut oil, divided
- Optional garnish: sliced green onions, chopped cilantro, sesame seeds

Instructions:

Preheat your oven to 400°F (200°C). Line a baking sheet with parchment paper or lightly grease it with cooking spray.

In a small saucepan, combine all the ingredients for the coconut glaze: coconut milk, soy sauce or tamari, honey or maple syrup, lime juice, grated ginger, minced garlic, chili flakes (if using), salt, and pepper. Heat over medium heat, stirring occasionally, until the mixture comes to a simmer. Reduce the heat to low and let it simmer for 2-3 minutes, stirring frequently, until slightly thickened. Remove the saucepan from the heat and set aside.

Season the salmon fillets with salt and pepper on both sides.

In a large skillet, heat 1 tablespoon of coconut oil over medium-high heat. Once the oil is hot, add the salmon fillets to the skillet, skin-side down if using skin-on fillets. Cook for 3-4 minutes, or until the salmon easily releases from the skillet and the skin is crispy and golden brown. If using skinless fillets, cook for 2-3 minutes per side, or until browned.

Transfer the partially cooked salmon fillets to the prepared baking sheet, skin-side down if using skin-on fillets.

Brush the coconut glaze generously over the top of each salmon fillet, reserving some for later use.

Place the baking sheet in the preheated oven and bake the salmon for 8-10 minutes, or until the salmon is cooked through and flakes easily with a fork.

While the salmon is baking, heat the remaining tablespoon of coconut oil in the same skillet used to sear the salmon over medium heat.

Once hot, add any remaining coconut glaze to the skillet and cook for 1-2 minutes, stirring constantly, until slightly thickened.

Once the salmon is done baking, remove it from the oven and brush the remaining coconut glaze from the skillet over the top of each fillet.

Garnish the coconut glazed salmon with sliced green onions, chopped cilantro, and sesame seeds, if desired.

Serve the salmon hot with your favorite side dishes, such as rice, quinoa, or steamed vegetables.

Enjoy your flavorful and delicious coconut glazed salmon!

Coconut Sweet Potato Casserole

Ingredients:

For the sweet potato filling:

- 4 cups mashed sweet potatoes (about 3-4 large sweet potatoes)
- 1/2 cup coconut milk (canned or carton)
- 1/4 cup brown sugar
- 2 tablespoons unsalted butter, melted
- 1 teaspoon vanilla extract
- 1/2 teaspoon ground cinnamon
- 1/4 teaspoon ground nutmeg
- 1/4 teaspoon salt

For the coconut topping:

- 1 cup shredded coconut (sweetened or unsweetened)
- 1/2 cup chopped pecans or walnuts
- 1/3 cup brown sugar
- 2 tablespoons unsalted butter, melted
- 1/2 teaspoon ground cinnamon
- Pinch of salt

Instructions:

Preheat your oven to 350°F (175°C). Grease a 9x13-inch baking dish or casserole dish with butter or cooking spray.

In a large mixing bowl, combine the mashed sweet potatoes, coconut milk, brown sugar, melted butter, vanilla extract, ground cinnamon, ground nutmeg, and salt. Mix until well combined and smooth.

Transfer the sweet potato mixture to the prepared baking dish, spreading it out evenly with a spatula.

In a separate bowl, combine the shredded coconut, chopped pecans or walnuts, brown sugar, melted butter, ground cinnamon, and a pinch of salt. Mix until the ingredients are evenly distributed and coated.

Sprinkle the coconut topping evenly over the sweet potato mixture in the baking dish, covering it completely.

Cover the baking dish with aluminum foil and bake in the preheated oven for 20 minutes.

After 20 minutes, remove the foil and continue baking for an additional 10-15 minutes, or until the coconut topping is golden brown and the sweet potato filling is heated through.

Once done, remove the casserole from the oven and let it cool for a few minutes before serving.

Serve the coconut sweet potato casserole warm as a delicious side dish for Thanksgiving dinner, holiday gatherings, or any special occasion.

Enjoy the creamy and flavorful combination of sweet potatoes and coconut in this delightful casserole!

Coconut Cream Truffles

Ingredients:

For the truffle filling:

- 1 cup sweetened shredded coconut
- 1/2 cup coconut cream (from a can of full-fat coconut milk)
- 2 tablespoons coconut oil, melted
- 1/4 cup powdered sugar
- 1/2 teaspoon vanilla extract
- Pinch of salt

For coating:

- 1 cup shredded coconut (sweetened or unsweetened), for rolling
- 4 ounces dark chocolate, chopped (optional, for dipping)

Instructions:

In a food processor, combine the sweetened shredded coconut, coconut cream, melted coconut oil, powdered sugar, vanilla extract, and a pinch of salt. Process until the mixture comes together and forms a thick, creamy dough.

Transfer the coconut mixture to a bowl and refrigerate it for about 30 minutes to firm up slightly.

Once the mixture is chilled, use a spoon or a small cookie scoop to scoop out portions of the mixture and roll them into small balls, about 1 inch in diameter, using your hands. Place the rolled balls on a baking sheet lined with parchment paper.

Place the shredded coconut for rolling in a shallow bowl or plate.

Roll each coconut ball in the shredded coconut until fully coated, pressing gently to adhere the coconut to the surface.

Once all the coconut balls are coated, return them to the baking sheet and refrigerate them for another 30 minutes to firm up further.

If dipping in chocolate, melt the dark chocolate in a microwave-safe bowl in 30-second intervals, stirring between each interval until smooth and fully melted.

Dip each chilled coconut ball into the melted chocolate, using a fork or dipping tool to fully coat it. Tap off any excess chocolate and place the dipped truffle back onto the parchment-lined baking sheet.

Once all the truffles are dipped in chocolate, return them to the refrigerator to allow the chocolate coating to set, about 15-20 minutes.

Once the chocolate coating is set, the coconut cream truffles are ready to serve. Enjoy these decadent and creamy coconut cream truffles as a delightful treat or gift for any occasion!

Store any leftover truffles in an airtight container in the refrigerator for up to one week.

Allow them to come to room temperature for a few minutes before serving, as they are best enjoyed slightly softened.

Coconut Pesto Pasta

Ingredients:

For the coconut pesto sauce:

- 1 cup fresh basil leaves, packed
- 1/2 cup unsweetened shredded coconut
- 1/4 cup pine nuts or almonds
- 2 cloves garlic, peeled
- 1/4 cup extra-virgin olive oil
- 2 tablespoons coconut milk (canned or carton)
- 1 tablespoon fresh lime juice
- Salt and pepper to taste

For the pasta:

- 12 ounces pasta of your choice (such as spaghetti, fettuccine, or penne)
- Salt for boiling water
- Optional toppings: grated Parmesan cheese, additional shredded coconut, cherry tomatoes, fresh basil leaves

Instructions:

Bring a large pot of salted water to a boil. Cook the pasta according to the package instructions until al dente. Drain the cooked pasta, reserving about 1/2 cup of pasta water, and set aside.

While the pasta is cooking, prepare the coconut pesto sauce. In a food processor or blender, combine the fresh basil leaves, shredded coconut, pine nuts or almonds, garlic cloves, extra-virgin olive oil, coconut milk, and lime juice. Blend until smooth and well combined. If the pesto is too thick, you can add a little more olive oil or coconut milk to reach your desired consistency. Season with salt and pepper to taste.

In a large skillet or saucepan, heat the prepared coconut pesto sauce over medium heat until warmed through, stirring occasionally.

Add the cooked pasta to the skillet with the warm coconut pesto sauce, tossing to coat the pasta evenly. If the sauce is too thick, you can add a splash of reserved pasta water to loosen it up.

Once the pasta is coated in the coconut pesto sauce and heated through, remove the skillet from the heat.
Serve the coconut pesto pasta hot, garnished with grated Parmesan cheese, additional shredded coconut, cherry tomatoes, and fresh basil leaves if desired. Enjoy your creamy and flavorful coconut pesto pasta as a delicious and satisfying meal!

Feel free to customize this recipe by adding grilled chicken, shrimp, or vegetables for added protein and nutrients. Adjust the ingredients according to your taste preferences and dietary needs.

Coconut Custard Pie

Ingredients:

For the pie crust:

- 1 1/4 cups all-purpose flour
- 1/2 teaspoon salt
- 1/2 cup unsalted butter, cold and cut into small cubes
- 3-4 tablespoons ice water

For the custard filling:

- 1 cup coconut milk
- 1 cup whole milk
- 1/2 cup granulated sugar
- 1/4 cup cornstarch
- 4 large eggs
- 1 teaspoon vanilla extract
- 1/2 cup sweetened shredded coconut, plus extra for garnish
- Pinch of salt

Instructions:

Preheat your oven to 375°F (190°C).

In a mixing bowl, combine the all-purpose flour and salt for the pie crust. Add the cold cubed butter and use a pastry cutter or fork to cut the butter into the flour until the mixture resembles coarse crumbs.

Gradually add the ice water, one tablespoon at a time, mixing with a fork until the dough just comes together. Be careful not to overwork the dough. Form the dough into a ball, flatten it into a disc, wrap it in plastic wrap, and refrigerate it for at least 30 minutes.

Roll out the chilled dough on a lightly floured surface into a circle about 12 inches in diameter. Carefully transfer the rolled-out dough to a 9-inch pie dish. Trim any excess dough hanging over the edges and crimp the edges with your fingers or a fork. Prick the bottom of the crust with a fork to prevent bubbling.

Line the pie crust with parchment paper or aluminum foil and fill it with pie weights or dried beans. Blind bake the crust in the preheated oven for 15 minutes. Remove the parchment paper and pie weights, then bake for an additional 5-7 minutes, or until the crust is lightly golden brown. Remove from the oven and let it cool slightly while you prepare the filling.

In a saucepan, combine the coconut milk, whole milk, granulated sugar, cornstarch, eggs, vanilla extract, and a pinch of salt for the custard filling. Whisk until smooth and well combined.

Place the saucepan over medium heat and cook the custard mixture, stirring constantly, until it thickens and comes to a gentle boil, about 5-7 minutes. Remove from heat and stir in the sweetened shredded coconut.

Pour the coconut custard filling into the partially baked pie crust. Smooth the top with a spatula and sprinkle with additional sweetened shredded coconut for garnish.

Return the pie to the oven and bake for 25-30 minutes, or until the custard is set and the top is lightly golden brown.

Once done, remove the pie from the oven and let it cool completely on a wire rack before slicing and serving.

Serve your delicious coconut custard pie at room temperature or chilled, and enjoy!

You can serve this pie as is or with a dollop of whipped cream or a scoop of vanilla ice cream for added indulgence.

Coconut Key Lime Bars

Ingredients:

For the crust:

- 1 1/2 cups graham cracker crumbs
- 1/4 cup granulated sugar
- 1/2 cup unsalted butter, melted

For the filling:

- 4 large egg yolks
- 1 can (14 ounces) sweetened condensed milk
- 1/2 cup key lime juice (freshly squeezed or bottled)
- Zest of 1 lime
- 1/2 cup sweetened shredded coconut

For the topping (optional):

- 1/2 cup sweetened shredded coconut, toasted
- Whipped cream or whipped coconut cream, for serving (optional)

Instructions:

Preheat your oven to 350°F (175°C). Line an 8x8-inch baking pan with parchment paper, leaving some overhang on the sides for easy removal.
In a mixing bowl, combine the graham cracker crumbs, granulated sugar, and melted butter for the crust. Stir until the mixture resembles wet sand.
Press the crust mixture firmly and evenly into the bottom of the prepared baking pan.
Bake the crust in the preheated oven for 10 minutes. Remove from the oven and let it cool slightly while you prepare the filling.
In another mixing bowl, whisk together the egg yolks and sweetened condensed milk until smooth.
Gradually add the key lime juice and lime zest to the egg mixture, whisking until well combined.

Stir in the sweetened shredded coconut until evenly distributed throughout the filling mixture.

Pour the filling over the partially baked crust in the baking pan, spreading it out evenly with a spatula.

Return the pan to the oven and bake for an additional 15-18 minutes, or until the filling is set and the edges are lightly golden brown.

Remove the pan from the oven and let the bars cool completely at room temperature. Then, refrigerate them for at least 2 hours to chill and set.

Once chilled, lift the bars out of the pan using the parchment paper overhang. Transfer them to a cutting board and cut into squares or bars.

If desired, sprinkle the toasted sweetened shredded coconut over the top of the bars before serving.

Serve the coconut key lime bars chilled, optionally topped with whipped cream or whipped coconut cream.

Enjoy these refreshing and tropical treats as a delightful dessert or snack!

Coconut Fried Rice

Ingredients:

- 2 cups cooked rice (preferably day-old rice, cooled)
- 2 tablespoons coconut oil or vegetable oil
- 2 cloves garlic, minced
- 1 small onion, diced
- 1 red bell pepper, diced
- 1 carrot, diced
- 1 cup frozen peas, thawed
- 3 green onions, chopped
- 2 eggs, lightly beaten
- 1/4 cup coconut milk
- 2 tablespoons soy sauce or tamari
- 1 tablespoon fish sauce (optional)
- 1 teaspoon curry powder
- Salt and pepper to taste
- 1/4 cup chopped fresh cilantro (optional, for garnish)
- Lime wedges (optional, for serving)

Instructions:

Heat 1 tablespoon of coconut oil in a large skillet or wok over medium heat.
Add the minced garlic and diced onion to the skillet and sauté for 2-3 minutes, until fragrant and softened.
Stir in the diced bell pepper and carrot, and cook for another 3-4 minutes, until the vegetables are tender-crisp.
Push the vegetables to one side of the skillet and add the beaten eggs to the other side. Scramble the eggs until cooked through, then mix them with the cooked vegetables.
Add the cooked rice to the skillet, breaking up any clumps with a spoon or spatula.
Pour the coconut milk, soy sauce or tamari, and fish sauce (if using) over the rice. Sprinkle the curry powder over the rice and toss everything together until evenly combined.

Stir in the thawed peas and chopped green onions, and continue to cook for another 2-3 minutes, until the peas are heated through and the rice is well coated with the sauce.

Season the coconut fried rice with salt and pepper to taste, adjusting the seasoning as needed.

Remove the skillet from the heat and transfer the coconut fried rice to serving plates or bowls.

Garnish with chopped fresh cilantro, if desired, and serve with lime wedges on the side for squeezing over the rice.

Enjoy your delicious and aromatic coconut fried rice as a flavorful main dish or side dish!

Feel free to customize this recipe by adding other vegetables or protein sources such as shrimp, chicken, or tofu. Adjust the seasonings according to your taste preferences and dietary needs.

Coconut Cilantro Lime Sauce

Ingredients:

- 1/2 cup coconut milk (canned or carton)
- 1/4 cup fresh cilantro leaves, packed
- 2 tablespoons lime juice (about 1 lime)
- 1 clove garlic, minced
- 1 tablespoon honey or maple syrup (optional, for sweetness)
- 1 tablespoon soy sauce or tamari
- 1 teaspoon grated ginger
- Pinch of red pepper flakes (optional, for heat)
- Salt and pepper to taste

Instructions:

In a blender or food processor, combine the coconut milk, fresh cilantro leaves, lime juice, minced garlic, honey or maple syrup (if using), soy sauce or tamari, grated ginger, and a pinch of red pepper flakes (if using).
Blend the ingredients until smooth and well combined. If the sauce is too thick, you can add a little water or more coconut milk to reach your desired consistency.
Taste the sauce and season with salt and pepper to taste. Adjust the sweetness or acidity by adding more honey or lime juice if necessary.
Once the sauce is well seasoned and blended to your liking, transfer it to a serving bowl or container.
Serve the coconut cilantro lime sauce immediately, or refrigerate it for later use. The flavors will meld together even more if left to chill for a few hours before serving.
Enjoy your delicious and versatile coconut cilantro lime sauce as a dipping sauce for spring rolls, grilled shrimp, chicken skewers, or vegetables. You can also use it as a marinade or dressing for salads, wraps, tacos, or bowls.

Feel free to customize this sauce by adding other ingredients like chopped jalapeño for extra heat, or coconut sugar for additional sweetness. Adjust the ingredients according to your taste preferences and dietary needs.

Coconut Pineapple Upside-Down Cake

Ingredients:

For the topping:

- 1/4 cup unsalted butter
- 1/2 cup brown sugar, packed
- 1 can (20 oz) pineapple slices, drained
- Maraschino cherries (optional), for garnish

For the cake batter:

- 1 1/2 cups all-purpose flour
- 1 teaspoon baking powder
- 1/4 teaspoon baking soda
- 1/4 teaspoon salt
- 1/2 cup unsalted butter, softened
- 1 cup granulated sugar
- 2 large eggs
- 1 teaspoon vanilla extract
- 1/2 cup coconut milk (canned or carton)
- 1/4 cup pineapple juice (reserved from draining pineapple slices)

Instructions:

Preheat your oven to 350°F (175°C). Grease a 9-inch round cake pan and line the bottom with parchment paper for easy removal.
In a small saucepan, melt the 1/4 cup of unsalted butter over medium heat. Once melted, add the brown sugar and stir until dissolved and bubbly, about 2-3 minutes.
Pour the melted butter and brown sugar mixture into the prepared cake pan, spreading it out evenly across the bottom.
Arrange the pineapple slices over the caramelized sugar mixture in the cake pan. Place maraschino cherries in the centers of the pineapple slices, if desired.
In a medium mixing bowl, sift together the all-purpose flour, baking powder, baking soda, and salt. Set aside.

In a large mixing bowl, cream together the softened butter and granulated sugar until light and fluffy.

Beat in the eggs, one at a time, until well incorporated. Add the vanilla extract and mix until combined.

Gradually add the dry flour mixture to the wet ingredients, alternating with the coconut milk and pineapple juice, beginning and ending with the dry ingredients. Mix until just combined, being careful not to overmix.

Pour the cake batter over the arranged pineapple slices in the cake pan, spreading it out evenly.

Bake the cake in the preheated oven for 40-45 minutes, or until a toothpick inserted into the center comes out clean and the top is golden brown.

Remove the cake from the oven and let it cool in the pan for 10 minutes.

After cooling, carefully invert the cake onto a serving platter or plate. Peel off the parchment paper, revealing the beautiful pineapple topping.

Allow the cake to cool completely before slicing and serving.

Serve the coconut pineapple upside-down cake slices with whipped cream or vanilla ice cream, if desired.

Enjoy your delicious and tropical dessert with its caramelized pineapple topping and moist coconut-infused cake!

Coconut Flour Brownies

Ingredients:

- 1/2 cup coconut oil, melted
- 1 cup coconut sugar or granulated sugar
- 3 large eggs
- 1 teaspoon vanilla extract
- 1/2 cup coconut flour
- 1/2 cup unsweetened cocoa powder
- 1/4 teaspoon salt
- 1/2 cup chocolate chips (optional)

Instructions:

Preheat your oven to 350°F (175°C). Grease an 8x8-inch baking pan or line it with parchment paper for easy removal.
In a large mixing bowl, whisk together the melted coconut oil and coconut sugar until well combined.
Add the eggs and vanilla extract to the bowl, and whisk until smooth and creamy.
In a separate bowl, sift together the coconut flour, cocoa powder, and salt.
Gradually add the dry ingredients to the wet ingredients, stirring until fully combined and no lumps remain.
If desired, fold in the chocolate chips until evenly distributed throughout the batter.
Pour the brownie batter into the prepared baking pan, spreading it out evenly with a spatula.
Bake in the preheated oven for 20-25 minutes, or until the edges are set and a toothpick inserted into the center comes out with a few moist crumbs attached.
Remove the brownies from the oven and let them cool completely in the pan on a wire rack.
Once cooled, slice the brownies into squares and serve.
Enjoy your delicious and fudgy coconut flour brownies as a tasty treat!

These brownies are rich, chocolatey, and gluten-free, making them a perfect indulgence for any occasion. Store any leftovers in an airtight container at room temperature for up to 3 days, or in the refrigerator for longer freshness.

Coconut Curry Lentil Soup

Ingredients:

- 1 tablespoon coconut oil or vegetable oil
- 1 onion, diced
- 3 cloves garlic, minced
- 1 tablespoon grated ginger
- 2 carrots, diced
- 2 celery stalks, diced
- 1 bell pepper, diced
- 1 cup dried red lentils, rinsed and drained
- 4 cups vegetable broth or chicken broth
- 1 can (14 ounces) coconut milk
- 2 tablespoons curry powder
- 1 teaspoon ground cumin
- 1/2 teaspoon ground turmeric
- 1/4 teaspoon cayenne pepper (optional, for heat)
- Salt and pepper to taste
- Juice of 1 lime
- Fresh cilantro, chopped (optional, for garnish)

Instructions:

Heat the coconut oil in a large pot or Dutch oven over medium heat.
Add the diced onion to the pot and sauté for 3-4 minutes, until softened and translucent.
Stir in the minced garlic and grated ginger, and cook for an additional 1-2 minutes, until fragrant.
Add the diced carrots, celery, and bell pepper to the pot, and cook for 5-7 minutes, until the vegetables are slightly softened.
Stir in the rinsed and drained red lentils, vegetable or chicken broth, coconut milk, curry powder, ground cumin, ground turmeric, and cayenne pepper (if using).
Bring the soup to a boil, then reduce the heat to low and simmer, covered, for 20-25 minutes, or until the lentils and vegetables are tender.
Season the soup with salt and pepper to taste. Adjust the seasoning as needed.
Stir in the lime juice to brighten the flavors of the soup.

If desired, use an immersion blender to partially blend the soup for a creamier texture, leaving some lentils and vegetables whole.

Ladle the coconut curry lentil soup into bowls and garnish with chopped fresh cilantro, if desired.

Serve the soup hot, accompanied by crusty bread or naan for dipping.

Enjoy your flavorful and comforting coconut curry lentil soup!

This soup is vegetarian, vegan, and gluten-free, making it a versatile and nutritious option for a satisfying meal. Store any leftovers in an airtight container in the refrigerator for up to 3-4 days.

Coconut Cream Cheese Frosting

Ingredients:

- 8 ounces (1 block) cream cheese, softened
- 1/2 cup unsalted butter, softened
- 2 cups powdered sugar
- 1/2 cup unsweetened shredded coconut
- 1 teaspoon vanilla extract
- Pinch of salt

Instructions:

In a mixing bowl, beat the softened cream cheese and butter together until smooth and creamy, using a hand mixer or stand mixer with the paddle attachment.
Gradually add the powdered sugar to the cream cheese mixture, mixing on low speed until fully incorporated and smooth.
Add the vanilla extract and a pinch of salt to the frosting, and continue to beat until well combined.
Fold in the unsweetened shredded coconut until evenly distributed throughout the frosting.
Once all the ingredients are well combined and the frosting is smooth, taste and adjust the sweetness or flavoring as desired.
Use the coconut cream cheese frosting to frost cakes, cupcakes, cookies, or any other baked goods of your choice.
Store any leftover frosting in an airtight container in the refrigerator for up to one week. Before using, let it come to room temperature and give it a quick stir to soften it up.
Enjoy your delicious and creamy coconut cream cheese frosting on your favorite desserts!

Feel free to adjust the amount of powdered sugar and shredded coconut according to your taste preferences. You can also add a splash of coconut milk or cream if you prefer a thinner consistency for spreading or piping.

Coconut Lime Shrimp Tacos

Ingredients:

For the Coconut Lime Shrimp:

- 1 pound large shrimp, peeled and deveined
- 1/2 cup coconut milk
- Zest and juice of 2 limes
- 2 cloves garlic, minced
- 1 tablespoon soy sauce
- 1 tablespoon honey or maple syrup
- Salt and pepper to taste
- 2 tablespoons coconut oil (for cooking)

For the Tacos:

- 8 small flour or corn tortillas
- Shredded lettuce or cabbage
- Diced tomatoes
- Sliced avocado
- Chopped cilantro
- Lime wedges for serving
- Optional: sliced jalapeños for extra heat

Instructions:

1. Marinate the Shrimp:

    In a bowl, combine coconut milk, lime zest, lime juice, minced garlic, soy sauce, honey or maple syrup, salt, and pepper.
    Add the shrimp to the marinade and toss until evenly coated. Let it marinate for at least 15-20 minutes in the refrigerator.

2. Cook the Shrimp:

    Heat coconut oil in a large skillet over medium-high heat.
    Once the skillet is hot, add the marinated shrimp in a single layer.
    Cook the shrimp for 2-3 minutes on each side until they turn pink and opaque. Be careful not to overcook.
    Once cooked, remove the shrimp from the skillet and set them aside.

3. Assemble the Tacos:

    Warm the tortillas in a separate skillet or in the oven.
    Place a spoonful of shredded lettuce or cabbage on each tortilla.
    Top with the cooked shrimp.
    Add diced tomatoes, sliced avocado, chopped cilantro, and sliced jalapeños if using.
    Serve the tacos with lime wedges on the side.

4. Serve and Enjoy:

    Serve the coconut lime shrimp tacos immediately.
    Squeeze fresh lime juice over the tacos just before eating for an extra burst of flavor.

Enjoy your delicious coconut lime shrimp tacos!

Coconut Pumpkin Soup

Ingredients:

- 2 tablespoons coconut oil or olive oil
- 1 onion, chopped
- 3 cloves garlic, minced
- 1 tablespoon grated ginger
- 1 teaspoon ground turmeric
- 1 teaspoon ground cumin
- 1/2 teaspoon ground coriander
- 1/4 teaspoon cayenne pepper (optional, for heat)
- 1 can (15 ounces) pumpkin puree (or about 2 cups homemade pumpkin puree)
- 1 can (13.5 ounces) coconut milk
- 3 cups vegetable or chicken broth
- 1 tablespoon maple syrup or honey
- Salt and pepper to taste
- Fresh cilantro or parsley, chopped (for garnish)
- Toasted pumpkin seeds (pepitas) for garnish (optional)

Instructions:

1. Sauté Aromatics:

    Heat coconut oil in a large pot over medium heat.
    Add chopped onion and sauté until translucent, about 5 minutes.
    Add minced garlic and grated ginger, and sauté for another 1-2 minutes until fragrant.

2. Add Spices and Pumpkin:

    Stir in ground turmeric, ground cumin, ground coriander, and cayenne pepper (if using).
    Cook for 1 minute to toast the spices.
    Add the pumpkin puree to the pot and stir to combine with the spices and aromatics.

3. Simmer the Soup:

    Pour in the coconut milk and vegetable or chicken broth. Stir well to combine.
    Bring the soup to a simmer over medium heat.
    Reduce the heat to low and let the soup simmer gently for about 15-20 minutes to allow the flavors to meld together.

4. Season and Blend:

Once the soup has simmered, remove it from the heat.
Stir in maple syrup or honey to balance the flavors.
Season with salt and pepper to taste.
Using an immersion blender or regular blender, carefully blend the soup until smooth and creamy. Be cautious when blending hot liquids.

5. Serve:

Ladle the coconut pumpkin soup into bowls.
Garnish with chopped fresh cilantro or parsley and toasted pumpkin seeds (pepitas) if desired.
Serve hot and enjoy!

This coconut pumpkin soup is best served fresh, but you can store any leftovers in an airtight container in the refrigerator for up to 3-4 days. Reheat gently on the stovetop or in the microwave before serving.

Coconut Lime Bars

Ingredients:

For the Crust:

- 1 1/2 cups graham cracker crumbs (about 10-12 graham crackers)
- 1/4 cup granulated sugar
- 1/2 cup unsalted butter, melted

For the Coconut Lime Filling:

- 4 large eggs
- 1 cup granulated sugar
- Zest of 2 limes
- 1/2 cup freshly squeezed lime juice (about 3-4 limes)
- 1/4 cup all-purpose flour
- 1/2 teaspoon baking powder
- 1/4 teaspoon salt
- 1 cup shredded coconut (sweetened or unsweetened)

For Garnish (Optional):

- Powdered sugar for dusting
- Lime zest

Instructions:

1. Preheat the Oven:

    Preheat your oven to 350°F (175°C).
    Grease a 9x9-inch baking dish or line it with parchment paper, leaving some overhang for easy removal.

2. Prepare the Crust:

    In a medium bowl, combine graham cracker crumbs, granulated sugar, and melted butter.
    Stir until the mixture resembles coarse sand and holds together when pressed.
    Press the mixture firmly and evenly into the bottom of the prepared baking dish.

3. Bake the Crust:

Bake the crust in the preheated oven for 10-12 minutes, or until it is lightly golden and set.

Remove from the oven and allow it to cool slightly while you prepare the filling.

4. Prepare the Coconut Lime Filling:

    In a large bowl, whisk together eggs and granulated sugar until well combined.
    Add lime zest and lime juice to the egg mixture, and whisk until smooth.
    In a separate small bowl, sift together flour, baking powder, and salt.
    Gradually add the flour mixture to the egg mixture, whisking until smooth and well combined.
    Fold in the shredded coconut until evenly distributed.

5. Assemble and Bake:

    Pour the coconut lime filling over the baked crust, spreading it out evenly.
    Return the baking dish to the oven and bake for 20-25 minutes, or until the filling is set and the edges are lightly golden.
    Remove from the oven and allow the bars to cool completely in the baking dish on a wire rack.

6. Garnish and Serve:

    Once cooled, you can optionally dust the bars with powdered sugar and sprinkle with additional lime zest for extra flavor and decoration.
    Use the parchment paper overhang to lift the bars out of the baking dish onto a cutting board.
    Cut into squares or bars using a sharp knife.
    Serve and enjoy these delicious coconut lime bars!

These bars can be stored in an airtight container in the refrigerator for up to 3-4 days. They also freeze well for longer storage. Simply wrap individual bars or the whole batch tightly in plastic wrap and then aluminum foil before freezing. Allow them to thaw in the refrigerator before serving.

Coconut Crème Brûlée

Ingredients:

- 2 cups heavy cream
- 1 cup coconut milk (full-fat)
- 1/2 cup granulated sugar, plus extra for caramelizing
- 6 large egg yolks
- 1 teaspoon vanilla extract
- 1/2 cup shredded coconut (sweetened or unsweetened), toasted (for garnish)

Instructions:

1. Preheat the Oven:

    Preheat your oven to 325°F (160°C).
    Place six ramekins in a deep baking dish or roasting pan. Set aside.

2. Prepare the Custard:

    In a medium saucepan, combine the heavy cream, coconut milk, and 1/2 cup of granulated sugar.
    Heat the mixture over medium heat, stirring occasionally, until it just begins to simmer. Do not boil.
    In a separate bowl, whisk together the egg yolks and vanilla extract until well combined.
    Slowly pour the hot cream mixture into the egg yolks, whisking constantly to temper the eggs.

3. Strain the Mixture:

    Strain the custard mixture through a fine-mesh sieve into a clean bowl to remove any lumps or bits of cooked egg.
    Divide the custard evenly among the prepared ramekins.

4. Bake the Custards:

    Carefully pour hot water into the baking dish or roasting pan around the ramekins until it reaches about halfway up the sides of the ramekins.
    Place the baking dish in the preheated oven and bake for 35-40 minutes, or until the custards are set around the edges but still slightly jiggly in the center.
    Remove the baking dish from the oven and carefully transfer the ramekins to a wire rack to cool completely.

Once cooled, cover the ramekins with plastic wrap and refrigerate for at least 2 hours, or until well chilled.

5. Caramelize the Sugar:

Just before serving, sprinkle a thin, even layer of granulated sugar over the top of each custard.
Using a kitchen torch, carefully melt and caramelize the sugar until it forms a golden-brown crust. Alternatively, you can place the ramekins under a broiler for 1-2 minutes, watching carefully to prevent burning.
Allow the caramelized sugar to cool and harden for a minute before serving.

6. Garnish and Serve:

Garnish each coconut crème brûlée with a sprinkle of toasted shredded coconut.
Serve immediately and enjoy the creamy, coconut-infused delight!

These coconut crème brûlée desserts are best served fresh and warm, with the caramelized sugar providing a satisfying crunch contrasted with the smooth custard.

Coconut Sesame Chicken

Ingredients:

For the Chicken:

- 1 pound boneless, skinless chicken breasts or thighs, cut into bite-sized pieces
- 1/2 cup all-purpose flour
- Salt and pepper to taste
- 2 eggs, beaten
- 1 cup shredded coconut (sweetened or unsweetened)
- 1/2 cup breadcrumbs (optional, for added crunch)
- Cooking oil for frying

For the Sauce:

- 1/4 cup soy sauce
- 2 tablespoons honey or maple syrup
- 2 tablespoons rice vinegar
- 1 tablespoon sesame oil
- 2 cloves garlic, minced
- 1 teaspoon grated ginger
- 1 tablespoon cornstarch
- 1/4 cup water
- Sesame seeds for garnish
- Chopped green onions for garnish

Instructions:

1. Prepare the Chicken:

> In a shallow bowl, mix together flour, salt, and pepper.
> In another shallow bowl, beat the eggs.
> In a third shallow bowl, combine shredded coconut and breadcrumbs (if using).
> Dip each piece of chicken into the flour mixture, then the beaten eggs, and finally coat evenly with the coconut mixture, pressing gently to adhere.

2. Fry the Chicken:

> Heat cooking oil in a large skillet or frying pan over medium-high heat.
> Once the oil is hot, add the coated chicken pieces in batches, making sure not to overcrowd the pan.

Fry the chicken for 3-4 minutes on each side, or until golden brown and cooked through. Remove the cooked chicken from the skillet and place them on a plate lined with paper towels to drain excess oil.

3. Make the Sauce:

In a small saucepan, whisk together soy sauce, honey or maple syrup, rice vinegar, sesame oil, minced garlic, and grated ginger.
In a separate bowl, mix cornstarch with water until well combined to create a slurry.
Add the cornstarch slurry to the saucepan with the sauce mixture.
Cook the sauce over medium heat, stirring constantly, until it thickens and reaches the desired consistency.

4. Combine and Serve:

Once the sauce has thickened, add the fried coconut sesame chicken to the saucepan.
Toss the chicken gently until evenly coated with the sauce.
Transfer the coated chicken to a serving plate.
Garnish with sesame seeds and chopped green onions.
Serve hot with steamed rice or your favorite side dishes.

Enjoy your delicious coconut sesame chicken! The crispy coconut coating paired with the savory-sweet sauce makes for a delightful meal.

Coconut Tres Leches Cake

Ingredients:

For the Cake:

- 1 cup all-purpose flour
- 1 1/2 teaspoons baking powder
- 1/4 teaspoon salt
- 5 large eggs, separated
- 1 cup granulated sugar, divided
- 1/3 cup whole milk
- 1 teaspoon vanilla extract
- 1/2 teaspoon coconut extract

For the Three Milks (Tres Leches):

- 1 can (14 ounces) sweetened condensed milk
- 1 can (12 ounces) evaporated milk
- 1 cup coconut milk (full-fat)

For the Topping:

- 2 cups whipped cream or whipped topping
- Shredded coconut for garnish

Instructions:

1. Preheat the Oven and Prepare the Pan:

    Preheat your oven to 350°F (175°C).
    Grease and flour a 9x13-inch baking pan and set aside.

2. Make the Cake:

    In a medium bowl, sift together flour, baking powder, and salt. Set aside.
    In a large bowl, beat egg yolks with 3/4 cup of granulated sugar until light and fluffy.
    Stir in milk, vanilla extract, and coconut extract until well combined.
    Gradually add the dry ingredients to the egg yolk mixture, stirring until smooth.

3. Whip the Egg Whites:

    In a separate clean bowl, beat egg whites until soft peaks form.
    Gradually add the remaining 1/4 cup of granulated sugar, beating until stiff peaks form.

4. Fold and Bake:

    Gently fold the whipped egg whites into the cake batter until just combined, being careful not to deflate the mixture.
    Pour the batter into the prepared baking pan and spread it out evenly.
    Bake in the preheated oven for 25-30 minutes or until a toothpick inserted into the center comes out clean.

5. Make the Three Milks Mixture:

    In a mixing bowl, combine sweetened condensed milk, evaporated milk, and coconut milk. Whisk until well combined.

6. Soak the Cake:

    Once the cake is baked and still warm, use a fork to poke holes all over the surface.
    Slowly pour the three milks mixture evenly over the cake, allowing it to soak in.

7. Chill the Cake:

    Cover the cake with plastic wrap and refrigerate for at least 4 hours or overnight to allow the flavors to meld and the cake to absorb the milk mixture.

8. Frost and Garnish:

    Before serving, spread whipped cream or whipped topping over the chilled cake.
    Sprinkle shredded coconut over the top for garnish.

9. Serve and Enjoy:

    Cut the coconut tres leches cake into squares and serve chilled.
    Enjoy the moist, flavorful, and indulgent dessert with friends and family!

This Coconut Tres Leches Cake is sure to be a hit at any gathering with its tropical twist on a classic favorite.

Coconut Flour Waffles

Ingredients:

- 4 large eggs, separated
- 1/4 cup coconut oil, melted
- 1/4 cup coconut milk
- 1/4 cup coconut flour
- 1 tablespoon honey or maple syrup (optional, for sweetness)
- 1/2 teaspoon baking powder
- Pinch of salt
- Optional toppings: fresh fruit, maple syrup, shredded coconut, whipped cream

Instructions:

1. Preheat the Waffle Iron:

    Preheat your waffle iron according to the manufacturer's instructions.

2. Separate Eggs:

    Separate the egg whites from the egg yolks and place them in separate bowls.

3. Prepare Batter:

    In a large mixing bowl, whisk together the egg yolks, melted coconut oil, coconut milk, and honey or maple syrup (if using) until well combined.
    In another bowl, combine the coconut flour, baking powder, and salt.
    Add the dry ingredients to the wet ingredients and mix until a smooth batter forms.

4. Whip Egg Whites:

    Using a hand mixer or stand mixer, beat the egg whites until stiff peaks form.

5. Combine Batter:

    Gently fold the whipped egg whites into the coconut flour batter until just combined. Be careful not to deflate the egg whites too much.

6. Cook Waffles:

    Lightly grease the preheated waffle iron with coconut oil or cooking spray.
    Pour enough batter onto the waffle iron to cover the surface (the amount will depend on the size of your waffle iron).

Close the waffle iron and cook the waffles according to the manufacturer's instructions, usually until golden brown and crispy.

7. Serve:

Once cooked, carefully remove the coconut flour waffles from the waffle iron and transfer them to a plate.
Serve the waffles warm with your favorite toppings, such as fresh fruit, maple syrup, shredded coconut, or whipped cream.

Enjoy your homemade coconut flour waffles! They're perfect for a leisurely breakfast or brunch, and their subtle coconut flavor adds a delicious twist to a classic dish.

Coconut Ginger Carrot Soup

Ingredients:

- 1 tablespoon coconut oil or olive oil
- 1 onion, chopped
- 2 cloves garlic, minced
- 1 tablespoon fresh ginger, grated
- 1 pound carrots, peeled and chopped
- 1 can (13.5 ounces) coconut milk
- 4 cups vegetable or chicken broth
- Salt and pepper to taste
- Optional garnishes: chopped fresh cilantro, toasted coconut flakes, drizzle of coconut milk

Instructions:

1. Sauté Aromatics:

    Heat the coconut oil or olive oil in a large pot over medium heat.
    Add the chopped onion and cook until translucent, about 5 minutes.
    Add the minced garlic and grated ginger, and cook for another 1-2 minutes until fragrant.

2. Cook Carrots:

    Add the chopped carrots to the pot and stir to combine with the aromatics.
    Cook for a few minutes, stirring occasionally.

3. Simmer Soup:

    Pour in the coconut milk and vegetable or chicken broth.
    Bring the mixture to a boil, then reduce the heat to low and let it simmer for about 15-20 minutes, or until the carrots are tender.

4. Blend Soup:

    Once the carrots are cooked, remove the pot from the heat.
    Using an immersion blender or regular blender, carefully blend the soup until smooth and creamy. Be cautious when blending hot liquids.

5. Season and Serve:

    Return the pot to the stove over low heat.

Season the soup with salt and pepper to taste, adjusting as needed.
If the soup is too thick, you can add more broth or coconut milk to reach your desired consistency.
Ladle the soup into bowls and garnish with chopped fresh cilantro, toasted coconut flakes, and a drizzle of coconut milk, if desired.

6. Enjoy:

Serve the coconut ginger carrot soup hot and enjoy its comforting flavors.

This soup is versatile and can be easily customized to suit your taste preferences. You can adjust the amount of ginger for a stronger or milder flavor, or add spices like curry powder or turmeric for extra depth. Enjoy!

Coconut Chocolate Chip Cookies

Ingredients:

- 1/2 cup (1 stick) unsalted butter, softened
- 1/2 cup granulated sugar
- 1/2 cup packed brown sugar
- 1 large egg
- 1 teaspoon vanilla extract
- 1 1/4 cups all-purpose flour
- 1/2 teaspoon baking soda
- 1/4 teaspoon salt
- 1 cup shredded coconut (sweetened or unsweetened)
- 1 cup semisweet chocolate chips

Instructions:

1. Preheat the Oven:

    Preheat your oven to 350°F (175°C).
    Line baking sheets with parchment paper or silicone baking mats. Set aside.

2. Cream Butter and Sugars:

    In a large mixing bowl, cream together the softened butter, granulated sugar, and brown sugar until light and fluffy.
    Add the egg and vanilla extract, and beat until well combined.

3. Mix Dry Ingredients:

    In a separate bowl, whisk together the all-purpose flour, baking soda, and salt.
    Gradually add the dry ingredients to the wet ingredients, mixing until just combined.

4. Add Coconut and Chocolate Chips:

    Fold in the shredded coconut and chocolate chips until evenly distributed throughout the cookie dough.

5. Scoop and Bake:

    Using a cookie scoop or spoon, drop rounded tablespoons of dough onto the prepared baking sheets, spacing them about 2 inches apart.

Optionally, press additional chocolate chips onto the tops of the dough balls for a more aesthetically pleasing appearance.

Bake in the preheated oven for 10-12 minutes, or until the cookies are golden brown around the edges.

Remove from the oven and let the cookies cool on the baking sheets for a few minutes before transferring them to a wire rack to cool completely.

6. Enjoy:

Once cooled, enjoy your delicious coconut chocolate chip cookies with a glass of milk or your favorite hot beverage.

These cookies can be stored in an airtight container at room temperature for several days.

They're perfect for snacking, dessert, or sharing with friends and family. Enjoy!

Coconut Curry Tofu

Ingredients:

- 14 oz (400g) firm tofu, drained and cubed
- 1 tablespoon coconut oil or vegetable oil
- 1 small onion, finely chopped
- 2 cloves garlic, minced
- 1 tablespoon fresh ginger, grated
- 2 tablespoons Thai red curry paste
- 1 can (13.5 oz / 400ml) full-fat coconut milk
- 1 tablespoon soy sauce or tamari
- 1 tablespoon brown sugar or maple syrup (optional, for sweetness)
- 1 tablespoon lime juice
- Salt and pepper to taste
- Fresh cilantro leaves, chopped, for garnish
- Cooked rice or noodles, for serving

Instructions:

1. Prepare the Tofu:

    Drain the tofu and gently press it between paper towels or kitchen towels to remove excess moisture.
    Cut the tofu into cubes and set aside.

2. Sauté Aromatics:

    Heat coconut oil or vegetable oil in a large skillet or wok over medium heat.
    Add the chopped onion, minced garlic, and grated ginger to the skillet. Sauté until the onion is soft and translucent, about 2-3 minutes.

3. Add Curry Paste:

    Stir in the Thai red curry paste and cook for another 1-2 minutes, until fragrant.

4. Cook Tofu:

    Add the cubed tofu to the skillet and gently toss to coat it with the curry paste mixture. Cook for a few minutes, stirring occasionally, to lightly brown the tofu on all sides.

5. Add Coconut Milk:

Pour in the full-fat coconut milk and stir to combine with the tofu and curry mixture. Bring the mixture to a simmer and let it cook for 5-7 minutes, allowing the flavors to meld together and the sauce to thicken slightly.

6. Season and Finish:

    Stir in the soy sauce or tamari, brown sugar or maple syrup (if using), and lime juice.
    Season with salt and pepper to taste.
    Cook for another 1-2 minutes, then remove the skillet from the heat.

7. Serve:

    Serve the coconut curry tofu hot, garnished with chopped cilantro leaves.
    Serve over cooked rice or noodles, if desired.

Enjoy your delicious coconut curry tofu! It's a flavorful and satisfying vegan dish that's perfect for weeknight dinners or entertaining guests.

Coconut Lime Rice

Ingredients:

- 1 cup long-grain white rice (such as jasmine or basmati)
- 1 cup canned coconut milk
- 1/2 cup water
- Zest of 1 lime
- Juice of 1 lime
- 1 tablespoon coconut oil or butter
- 1/2 teaspoon salt
- Optional: Fresh cilantro or shredded coconut for garnish

Instructions:

1. Rinse the Rice:

    Place the rice in a fine-mesh strainer and rinse it under cold water until the water runs clear. This helps remove excess starch and prevents the rice from becoming too sticky when cooked.

2. Cook the Rice:

    In a medium saucepan, combine the rinsed rice, canned coconut milk, water, lime zest, lime juice, coconut oil or butter, and salt.
    Bring the mixture to a boil over medium-high heat.
    Once boiling, reduce the heat to low, cover the saucepan with a tight-fitting lid, and let the rice simmer for 15-20 minutes, or until all the liquid is absorbed and the rice is tender.

3. Fluff the Rice:

    Once the rice is cooked, remove the saucepan from the heat and let it sit, covered, for 5 minutes.
    After 5 minutes, uncover the saucepan and use a fork to fluff the rice, separating the grains gently.

4. Garnish and Serve:

    Transfer the coconut lime rice to a serving dish.
    If desired, garnish with fresh cilantro leaves or shredded coconut for extra flavor and presentation.

Serve the coconut lime rice alongside your favorite main dishes, such as curries, grilled chicken or fish, or stir-fries.

Enjoy your delicious coconut lime rice as a flavorful and aromatic accompaniment to your meal!

Coconut Cream Donuts

Ingredients:

For the Donuts:

- 1 cup all-purpose flour
- 1/2 cup granulated sugar
- 1 teaspoon baking powder
- 1/4 teaspoon baking soda
- 1/4 teaspoon salt
- 1/2 cup coconut milk
- 1/4 cup coconut oil, melted
- 1 large egg
- 1 teaspoon vanilla extract

For the Glaze:

- 1 cup powdered sugar
- 2-3 tablespoons coconut milk
- 1/2 teaspoon vanilla extract
- Shredded coconut, for topping (optional)

Instructions:

1. Preheat the Oven:

    Preheat your oven to 350°F (175°C).
    Grease a donut pan with non-stick cooking spray or coconut oil. If you don't have a donut pan, you can use a mini muffin pan to make donut holes.

2. Prepare the Batter:

    In a large mixing bowl, whisk together the flour, sugar, baking powder, baking soda, and salt.
    In another bowl, whisk together the coconut milk, melted coconut oil, egg, and vanilla extract until well combined.
    Pour the wet ingredients into the dry ingredients and stir until just combined. Be careful not to overmix.

3. Fill the Donut Pan:

    Spoon the batter into a piping bag or a resealable plastic bag with the corner snipped off.

Pipe the batter into the prepared donut pan, filling each cavity about 2/3 full.

4. Bake the Donuts:

   Place the donut pan in the preheated oven and bake for 10-12 minutes, or until the donuts are lightly golden and spring back when lightly pressed.
   Remove the donut pan from the oven and let the donuts cool in the pan for a few minutes before transferring them to a wire rack to cool completely.

5. Make the Glaze:

   In a shallow bowl, whisk together the powdered sugar, coconut milk, and vanilla extract until smooth. Add more coconut milk if needed to achieve your desired consistency.
   Once the donuts are completely cooled, dip the tops of each donut into the glaze, allowing any excess to drip off.
   If desired, sprinkle shredded coconut over the glazed donuts for added texture and flavor.

6. Serve:

   Let the glaze set for a few minutes before serving the coconut cream donuts.
   Enjoy your delicious homemade treats!

These coconut cream donuts are best enjoyed fresh but can be stored in an airtight container at room temperature for up to 2 days.

Coconut Spinach Salad

Ingredients:

For the Salad:

- 6 cups fresh baby spinach leaves
- 1/2 cup shredded coconut (toasted if desired)
- 1/4 cup sliced almonds or chopped pecans
- 1/4 cup dried cranberries or raisins
- 1/4 cup sliced red onion (optional)
- 1 ripe avocado, diced (optional)

For the Dressing:

- 2 tablespoons coconut oil, melted
- 2 tablespoons extra virgin olive oil
- 2 tablespoons apple cider vinegar or white wine vinegar
- 1 tablespoon honey or maple syrup
- 1 tablespoon lime juice
- 1 teaspoon Dijon mustard
- Salt and pepper to taste

Instructions:

1. Prepare the Salad:

    Rinse the baby spinach leaves under cold water and pat them dry with paper towels or a salad spinner.
    In a large salad bowl, combine the baby spinach leaves, shredded coconut, sliced almonds or chopped pecans, dried cranberries or raisins, sliced red onion (if using), and diced avocado (if using). Toss gently to combine.

2. Make the Dressing:

    In a small bowl, whisk together the melted coconut oil, extra virgin olive oil, apple cider vinegar or white wine vinegar, honey or maple syrup, lime juice, and Dijon mustard until emulsified.
    Season the dressing with salt and pepper to taste.

3. Dress the Salad:

    Drizzle the dressing over the salad just before serving.

Toss the salad gently to coat the ingredients evenly with the dressing.

4. Serve:

Transfer the dressed coconut spinach salad to individual serving plates or bowls. Optionally, garnish with additional shredded coconut, sliced almonds or chopped pecans, and dried cranberries or raisins for extra texture and flavor.
Serve immediately and enjoy!

This coconut spinach salad is perfect as a side dish or as a light meal on its own. It's packed with nutrients and flavors that will delight your taste buds.

Coconut Chicken Satay

Ingredients:

For the Chicken Satay:

- 1 pound boneless, skinless chicken breasts or thighs, cut into thin strips
- 1/4 cup coconut milk
- 2 tablespoons soy sauce
- 2 tablespoons fish sauce
- 2 tablespoons lime juice
- 1 tablespoon brown sugar or honey
- 2 cloves garlic, minced
- 1 tablespoon curry powder
- 1 teaspoon ground turmeric
- Bamboo skewers, soaked in water for 30 minutes

For the Coconut Peanut Sauce:

- 1/2 cup creamy peanut butter
- 1/2 cup coconut milk
- 2 tablespoons soy sauce
- 1 tablespoon brown sugar or honey
- 1 tablespoon lime juice
- 1 teaspoon grated ginger
- 1 clove garlic, minced
- Crushed peanuts and chopped cilantro for garnish (optional)

Instructions:

1. Marinate the Chicken:

   In a bowl, whisk together the coconut milk, soy sauce, fish sauce, lime juice, brown sugar or honey, minced garlic, curry powder, and ground turmeric.
   Add the chicken strips to the marinade and toss until evenly coated. Cover and refrigerate for at least 1 hour, or overnight for best flavor.

2. Make the Coconut Peanut Sauce:

   In a small saucepan, combine the peanut butter, coconut milk, soy sauce, brown sugar or honey, lime juice, grated ginger, and minced garlic.

Heat the sauce over medium heat, stirring constantly, until the peanut butter is melted and the sauce is smooth and creamy. Remove from heat and set aside.

3. Skewer and Grill the Chicken:

   Preheat your grill to medium-high heat.
   Thread the marinated chicken strips onto the soaked bamboo skewers, leaving a little space between each piece.
   Grill the chicken skewers for 3-4 minutes per side, or until cooked through and nicely charred on the edges. Make sure to rotate the skewers for even cooking.

4. Serve:

   Arrange the grilled chicken satay skewers on a serving platter.
   Serve the coconut peanut sauce on the side for dipping or drizzle it over the skewers.
   Optionally, garnish with crushed peanuts and chopped cilantro for extra flavor and presentation.
   Serve the coconut chicken satay immediately and enjoy!

These coconut chicken satay skewers are perfect as an appetizer or main dish for parties, gatherings, or weeknight dinners. The combination of tender chicken and creamy coconut peanut sauce is sure to be a crowd-pleaser!

Coconut Matcha Latte

Ingredients:

- 1 teaspoon matcha green tea powder
- 1 tablespoon hot water (not boiling)
- 1 cup unsweetened coconut milk (or any milk of your choice)
- 1 tablespoon honey, maple syrup, or sweetener of choice (optional)
- Optional: Unsweetened shredded coconut or coconut flakes for garnish

Instructions:

1. Prepare the Matcha:

    In a small bowl or mug, add the matcha green tea powder.
    Pour in the hot water (not boiling) over the matcha powder.
    Use a bamboo whisk or a small whisk to whisk the matcha and water together until smooth and frothy. Set aside.

2. Heat the Coconut Milk:

    In a small saucepan, heat the coconut milk over medium heat until it is hot but not boiling. Alternatively, you can heat the coconut milk in the microwave for about 1-2 minutes until warm.

3. Mix the Latte:

    Once the coconut milk is heated, pour it into a mug.
    Add the prepared matcha mixture to the mug, stirring until well combined.
    If desired, sweeten the latte with honey, maple syrup, or your preferred sweetener, adjusting to taste.

4. Froth (Optional):

    If you have a milk frother, you can use it to froth the coconut matcha latte for an extra creamy texture. Simply froth the latte until it becomes frothy and well-mixed.

5. Garnish and Serve:

    Optionally, garnish the coconut matcha latte with unsweetened shredded coconut or coconut flakes for added flavor and presentation.

Serve the latte hot and enjoy its delicious and invigorating flavor!

This coconut matcha latte is perfect for starting your day with a boost of energy or for a cozy afternoon pick-me-up. Feel free to adjust the sweetness and coconut milk ratio to suit your taste preferences.